Words of Praise for
Hank Wesselman and His Books

"Hank Wesselman is that rare combination of visionary and scholar whose message has the ring of truth, clarity, and urgency. He is an expert guide who fully realizes that he is playing with scientific and spiritual dynamite."

— **Larry Dossey, M.D.,** author of
Reinventing Medicine and *Healing Words*

"Hank Wesselman's *Visionseeker* rivals the works of Carlos Castaneda."

— **Michael Harner, Ph.D.,** author of
The Way of the Shaman and director of the
Foundation for Shamanic Studies

THE
JOURNEY
to the
SACRED
GARDEN

Also by Hank Wesselman, Ph.D.

Spiritwalker:
Messages from the Future

Medicinemaker:
Mystic Encounters on the Shaman's Path

Visionseeker:
Shared Wisdom from the Place of Refuge

※ ※ ※

All of the above are available at your local bookstore.
Visionseeker may also be ordered through Hay House, Inc.:

Hay House USA: www.hayhouse.com®
Hay House Australia: www.hayhouse.com.au
Hay House UK: www.hayhouse.co.uk
Hay House South Africa: www.hayhouse.co.za
Hay House India: www.hayhouse.co.in

THE JOURNEY
to the
SACRED GARDEN

A Guide to Traveling in the Spiritual Realms

Hank Wesselman, Ph.D.

HAY HOUSE, INC.
Carlsbad, California • New York City
London • Sydney • Johannesburg
Vancouver • Hong Kong • New Delhi

Published and distributed in the United States by: Hay House, Inc.: www.hayhouse
.com® • **Published and distributed in Australia by:** Hay House Australia Pty. Ltd.:
www.hayhouse.com.au • **Published and distributed in the United Kingdom by:** Hay
House UK, Ltd.: www.hayhouse.co.uk • **Published and distributed in the Republic of
South Africa by:** Hay House SA (Pty), Ltd.: www.hayhouse.co.za • **Distributed in
Canada by:** Raincoast: www.raincoast.com • **Published in India by:** Hay House
Publishers India: www.hayhouse.co.in

Editorial supervision: Jill Kramer • *Design:* Ashley Brown

Library of Congress Cataloging-in-Publication Data

Wesselman, Henry Barnard.
     The journey to the sacred garden : a guide to traveling in the spiritual realms /
Hank Wesselman.
       p. cm.
       Includes bibliographical references.
     ISBN 1-40190-111-5
       1. Shamanism. 2. Shamans. 3. Spiritual life. I. Title.
     BF1611 .W4347 2003
     291.1'44—dc21

                                                                        2002011576

Tradepaper ISBN: 978-1-4019-4158-1

15 14 13 12   7 6 5 4
1st printing, January 2003
4th printing, July 2012

Printed in the United States of America

Contents

Acknowledgments

∫pecial thanks are due to Jill Kuykendall, my wise, lovely, and compassionate wife; and to Erica and Anna Wesselman, the wonderful children we created together.

Gratitude is also expressed to Kahu Nelita Anderson, Carolyn and Bob Blackstone, Tahdi Blackstone, Gregg Braden, Marguerite Craig, Frank DeMarco, Larry Dossey, Kathleen and Peter Golden, Stan Grof, Sandra and Michael Harner, Barbara Marx Hubbard, Sandra Ingerman, Robin and Cody Johnson, Ali'i Maraea Kahalopuna, Kahu Nainoa Kaneohe, Kapohaku'ki'ihele, Serge King, John Mack, Nina and Kahu Hale Kealohalani Makua, Eva and Mason Ma'ikui, Brooke Medicine Eagle, Ralph Metzner, Judith Orloff, Greta Lind Pizzo, Carolyn Precourt, Bruce and Carol Ritberger, Joanne and Ernest Reyes, Kahu Morrnah Simeona, Sanderson Sims, Susanne Sims, Sandy Tofflemire, Lili Townsend, Cynee and Bill Wenner, Mary Wright,

Sandra Wright, the members of the 4th West Coast Training Program with the Foundation for Shamanic Studies, as well as the Hawaiian spiritual warrior society, Na Ao Koa o Pu'u Kohola Heiau.

Thanks also to my literary agents, Candice Fuhrman and Linda Michaels; to my editor, Jill Kramer; and to Louise Hay, Reid Tracy, Jacqui Clark, Tonya Toone, Jeannie Liberati, Christy Salinas, Rocky George, and everyone else at Hay House.

1 The Awakening

My work as an anthropologist over the past several decades has led me to suspect that there are countless numbers of evolutionary sleepers out there in the mainstream of humanity, each containing within themselves an extraordinary biological-energetic program.

I've come to believe that this program is on our DNA, part of our genetic "hard drive," so to speak, and it's been my personal experience that when this program is "double-clicked," higher functions coded into the personal mind-body matrix may be awakened.

Our conscious awareness may expand dramatically in response, allowing us to have the direct, transpersonal connection with the sacred realms that defines the mystic. Needless to say, this is an experience that has transformed me utterly.

The inner fieldwork of the mystics suggests that "the program" is closely associated with the ductless glands, the brain, and the heart; and that these organs, in turn, are in relationship with the dense concentrations of energy known as chakras, located in the core of our personal etheric matrix. When these physical and energetic mission control centers are activated, the relationship between them can dramatically affect the body and the brain, which may undergo striking changes.[1]

At the time of this writing, humankind has not, as a whole, experienced the triggering of these higher functions, but those individuals who have could well be prototypes for a new kind of human. To be specific, the program may reveal who and what we may all become when we awaken from the consensual slumber of culture at large and are drawn across an evolutionary threshold to become a new species.[2]

This is not fantasy, but a real phenomenon known to science as *speciation*. When it happens rapidly, producing a sudden evolutionary jump, it's called *punctuated equilibrium*.

After countless eons of time during which the human body and brain have taken form in co-creative relationship with Nature and Spirit, we appear to be ready to engage in a truly extraordinary adventure—the evolution of consciousness.

In short, we're primed to experience the full expression of the human spectrum that is latent within us.

2 The Visionseekers

We live in interesting times. In addition to everything else going on in the Western world, there's a spiritual awakening quietly taking place, and right at its heart lies the discovery of that program within us—a program that when experienced directly, has the potential to precipitate undreamed-of levels of personal transformation.

In response, increasing numbers of modern scholars and spiritual seekers alike are reconsidering who we are as human beings and where we came from. And in doing so, we're rediscovering the ancient, time-tested methods for expanding consciousness that were pioneered tens of millennia ago by the shamans and mystics of the traditional peoples—techniques that are now known to be a form of technology—a technology of the sacred.

❊ ❊ ❊   ❊ ❊ ❊

3 The Technology of the Sacred

Traditional people in indigenous societies know their surrounding environments in great detail. If there are psychotropic plants growing nearby, the ritual use of hallucinogens derived from these "plant teachers" is sometimes utilized for the purpose of expanding awareness and accessing the sacred realms.

Many investigators have even suggested that the discovery and use of plant-derived *psychedelics* (meaning "mind-manifesting") may have been responsible for the development of spiritual awareness in human beings in the first place. By implication, hallucinogens may very well have served as the causation for the genesis of religion. Accordingly, an alternate term for these plant teachers is often used—the word *entheogen*—meaning "releasing the deity within."[3]

The growing literature on hallucinogens reveals striking cross-cultural similarities in the reported effects of these natural substances on human consciousness. These include the capacity to channel the energy of the universe, to discover the most profound secrets of nature, and to acquire wisdom that may be used for magical, medical, and religious purposes.

But equally powerful and far more widespread are the psychological and physiological methods developed by the traditional peoples for altering consciousness and repatterning it in specific ways—techniques such as fasting, sleep deprivation, physical exhaustion, hyperventilation, or even the experiencing of temperature extremes during rituals of purification such as the sweat lodge.[4]

It's also generally known that the intensely physical stimulus of monotonous drumming and rattling, combined with culturally meaningful ritual and ceremony, prayer and chant, and singing and dancing, can enable the shifting of consciousness into visionary modes of perception. Not surprisingly, the use of drums and rattles by sacred practitioners around the world is almost universal.

Until relatively recently, Westerners have tended to regard the whole issue of altered-state experiences as mysterious, paranormal, and even pathological—and some of us, in ignorance, still respond to the idea of expanded awareness and connection with spirits with fear and rejection.

By contrast, in a traditional society, each girl and boy grows up in relationship with elder ceremonial leaders and mystics who are able to access expanded states intentionally for the benefit of themselves and for others, or even for the entire community. The traditionals know that virtually everyone can learn how to access sacred states of consciousness to some extent, and that each of us is a potential holy person. They also know that some of us are real naturals at it.

With the double-clicking of the program, we become aware of our ability to perceive in an expanded way. And once activated, this ability improves and deepens with practice, allowing us to ascend toward the luminous horizon of our personal and collective destiny in a completely new way.

Today, this phenomenon can be partially understood in scientific terms. It's known, for example, that the nature of the visionary experience can be determined, to some extent, by our focused intentionality, by our belief systems, and by the set and setting in which we find ourselves. These serve as "repatterning forces" that can give new shapes to our mind-set, allowing the seeker to access many varieties of experience, including connection with the numinous dimensions of the spirit world . . . if that is their intention.

The traditional people also know a great secret: Any human activity or endeavor can be enormously enhanced through utilizing and eventually mastering this sacred technology. Another secret: If we go back far enough, we're all descended from indigenous tribal ancestors, Westerners and non-Westerners alike.

So let us now consider the tribal mystic in a bit more detail, for in doing so, we may learn something interesting about ourselves, as well as where we're headed.

4 The Shaman

When Westerners hear the word *shaman,* most of us tend to conjure up an image of a masked and costumed tribal person dancing around a fire in the dark, involved in some mysterious ritual, accompanied by drumbeats. Yet within that cultural shell of mask, costume, and ritual, there's a woman or man who possesses a set of very real skills.

All true shamans utilize aspects of sacred technology to double-click their program and expand their conscious awareness, allowing them to engage in visionary journeys into the inner dimensions of reality known as the Other World, the Spirit World, the Dreamtime, or simply, the Sacred.

Shamans are masters of trance. They dissociate aspects of their soul and literally "spiritwalk" into levels of the inner worlds where they encounter spirits—for example, the spirits of nature, the higher gods and goddesses, the spirits of their deceased ancestors, the ascended spiritual masters and angelic forces, or even those higher spirits beyond planetary and solar development. Based on their own direct experiences, shamans affirm with absolute confidence that these realities, as well as the spirits that they encounter within them, are real.

Accordingly, I've come to categorize this extraordinary ability as "the spiritwalker program."

5 The Spiritwalker Program

∫hamans tend to run in families, reinforcing the idea that the spiritwalker program may have a genetic foundation. This has led some investigators to suggest that a substantial portion of the general human population may possess it—a hypothesis that's supported by some anthropological field observations. Among the traditional Kalahari Bushmen, up to 50 percent of the men and 30 percent of the women could shamanize when the need required it.[5]

The ability to engage in visionary experience may be part of the hereditary birthright of all human beings everywhere, both traditionals and nontribal moderns alike. Seen from this perspective, the evolutionary sleepers among us are simply those who are unaware of the spiritwalker program's existence within them because they haven't experienced it yet.

I was one such sleeper until something double-clicked the program on my own inner hard drive, initiating a life-changing series of events that is recorded in my *Spiritwalker* trilogy.[6]

Through personal experience with the program, spirit-walkers become mystics, and through training, mystics can become shamans.

Several strongly held "knowns" can be found among virtually all shamans and spiritwalkers of the world, among them: (1) We can all draw upon mysterious, compassionate forces in the inner spiritual realms who are willing to help us in various ways; and (2) these sympathetic spirits are not all powerful—they need our help in opening up a bridge or channel between their reality and ours in order for them to be of service to us.[7]

Shamans are thus revealed as the visionary explorers and spiritual activists who can connect with the spirits, as well as with the power and wisdom that the spirits possess. Shamans are holy people who serve their communities as the bridge between the worlds, allowing them to bring the power back into our everyday reality in order to manifest various things.

6 The Shaman's Practice

Accomplished shamans do healing work on various levels, and interestingly, all agree that it is the spirits who do what is required, not themselves. These compassionate forces work with the shaman to help restore power to those who have lost it, for example, or they may help the shaman access concealed information of personal importance, a practice known as *divination*. The spirits may perform healing work on the physical, mental-emotional, and spiritual levels of being, restoring balance and harmony within a sufferer, and helping to repair the holes torn in the fabric of their soul.

Some shamans are accomplished at linking up with their team of spirits to recover soul parts lost through accident, trauma, or sometimes outright theft by "soul-stealers." Soul loss is recognizable as apathy, an absence of joy, an inability to feel love or receive it, suicidal tendencies, addictions, chronic despair, and depression. The shaman, in partnership with their spiritual allies, tracks the lost soul parts, finds them, and returns them to their original owners, a talent generally known as *soul retrieval*.

Some shamans become specialists in helping to convey the souls of the dead to where they're supposed to go in the afterlife, a skill called *psychopomp work*.

Proficiency in skills such as these sets the shaman apart from other kinds of religious practitioners, revealing them as medicinemakers and spiritual healers in whose capable hands both the physical and metaphysical equilibrium of their communities rest. When the bridge is formed, the miraculous happens. And this is true magic.

There are several important points here:

- Shamanism is not a religion.

- It's a spiritual method consisting of a body of techniques that allows us to activate the spiritwalker program within ourselves so that we, too, can travel into the spiritual realms where we may connect with our inner sources of power and wisdom.

This clearly reveals that "shamanism" does not have to conflict with the spiritual wisdom and teachings of any religious tradition. Indeed, if you look closely, it's there within them all. The shaman is the ancestor of our priestesses and priests, our rabbis and mullahs, our visionaries and mystics.

Different religious traditions describe this experience in different ways, but their conclusions are clearly the same. The Delphic oracle proclaimed: "Know thyself, and thou shalt know the Cosmos." Christianity tells us that "the Kingdom of Heaven is within you." In the words of Saint Clement: "He who knows himself knows God." Buddhism says: "Look within. Thou art Buddha." In Siddha Yoga, "God dwells within you as you." And in Islam, "He who knows himself knows his Lord."[8]

In the same breath, it should be observed that shamanism is not an exclusive tradition that can be known and practiced only by indigenous natives. As has been observed, all Westerners are descended from indigenous tribal peoples if we go back far enough, and those people had great shamans.

※ ※ ※　※ ※ ※

7 Our Visionary Tradition

The Druids, as well as the wizards and witches of the Celtic and Anglo-Saxon tribal peoples of Europe and the British Isles, were the last holders of the ancient shamanic wisdom tradition that predated the arrival of Christianity at the end of the Roman era. Scholars have affirmed that the word *witch* was originally a term of respect associated with superior knowledge and learning, as well as with "uncommon but not unlawful skills."[9] From the scant literature that survives from the medieval period, there's no evidence that witches were anything but powerful and effective healers.

Unfortunately, as the politically motivated priesthoods of the early Christian churches rose to power in the towns and cities of Europe and Britain during the Middle Ages (and later in the Americas), the democratic, individualist practices of the shamans of the countryside were suppressed, often ruthlessly. These rural "wise women of the woods" and the "men of power and knowledge" were the losers in a political battle over who had jurisdiction over the human soul—claimed by the church—and the human body, claimed by the newly incorporated guild of physicans and surgeons in 1518.

Hundreds of thousands and possibly millions of shamans were massacred in the ensuing holocaust of the great witch-hunt that reached its peak between 1500 and 1650. Recorded history reveals that this event actually began in the 12th century, and that the religious intolerance that fed this shameful debacle survives to this day in various guises. Not surprisingly, those who possess shamanic abilities in the West have tended to keep a low profile until relatively recently.

Many of us discovered as children that we had the shamanic program through our relationships with imaginary friends, or with the fairies of the woods and waterways of the wild places. But many may also stumble into it through enduring a life crisis—for example, a serious illness or trauma that may precipitate visions. Others may be drawn toward training workshops where their gifts may become apparent under the guidance of an accomplished teacher.

My many years of involvement with shamanic training workshops have revealed that the program can easily be reactivated in nontribal Westerners, even after a thousand years of dormancy. The anthropologist Michael Harner agrees. He and his colleagues have successfully trained tens of thousands in the shamanic method over the past several decades. He has suggested that about 90 percent of us possess shamanic abilities to some extent, with around 50 percent being real naturals at it.[10]

Interestingly, modern "shamanic work" does not necessitate a retreat into archaic traditions, nor are Western people, on the whole, interested in "playing Indian" or becoming "born-again aboriginals." While some are strongly drawn toward the psychospiritual worldview and symbology of this indigenous tradition or that, I suspect that something entirely new is actually coming into being.

And in the process, Western spirituality is being revitalized on an ever-increasing scale.

※ ※ ※　※ ※ ※

8 The Revitalization of Spirituality

It is of interest that the current spiritual reawakening is mainly happening outside the carefully patrolled borders of our organized religions. It appears to be cutting across socioeconomic levels of achievement and status, and is transcending cultural, political, and ethnic boundaries as well.[11] It's not surprising, therefore, that this widespread movement includes a growing revival of interest in shamanism.

By using the shamanic method, each person is gifted with their freedom, their sovereignty, and their right to develop spiritually. In doing so, each of us becomes our own teacher, our own priestess or priest, on our own prophet, enabling us to receive spiritual revelations directly from the highest sources—ourselves.

This is an appealing proposition to Westerners, and virtually everyone in the transformational community knows that it's possible to connect with the dimensional realities where all the mysteries, great and small, become known.

This is the direct path of the mystic at its absolute best. This is the sacred way that leads each of us into the experience of self-empowerment and self-perception, without the need for any particular organized religious or spiritual structure to do it for us.

In the same breath, let me add that it helps to have some structural foundation in the beginning, and most of us find one that fits—whether Islamic, Christian, Jewish, Hindu, Buddhist, or Jain.

The exploration of the nature of reality, as well as the mystery of who we are and what we're doing here, is the substrate of the quest. It's not about clearing up these mysteries. It's about making these mysteries clear.

When we experience the mysteries directly, we make them our own. And although it's possible to do this in the church or the temple, the zendo or the mosque, the challenge is to accomplish it out in the world at large—in the supermarket or the bank, the law office or the fast-food joint, in our families, in our friendships, and in our alliances. It is in this manner that we bring the mysteries into our everyday lives, and by association, into our relationships with everyone, everywhere—forever.

※ ※ ※　※ ※ ※

9 The Quest

At its inception, this inquiry into the mystery is intensely personal. Yet as it progresses, it leads the seeker inevitably toward a universal and ultimately altruistic perspective, one that takes us straight into the irreversible vortex of spiritual enlightenment. This progression, once begun, changes us profoundly and forever because it conveys to each of us the experience of authentic initiation.

This small book, with its accompanying compact disc (CD), may provide you with the key to opening your own inner portal into the sacred realms. Needless to say, it's not designed to replace the years of disciplined practice engaged in by traditional shamans in indigenous societies. But it may serve as a catalyst, as a bridge, helping you to embark upon your spiritual adventure, assisting you by double-clicking your spiritwalker program so that you may find your personal place of power and healing in the inner worlds.

※ ※ ※ ※ ※ ※

33

10 How to Use the Compact Disc

When I first began to visit the spiritual worlds in a structured, goal-oriented way, I utilized the sound of a rattle or drum to double-click my program and expand my awareness, allowing me greater ease in accessing the visionary levels that are so familiar to traditional shamans.

With practice, I discovered that I could settle into a gentle wrist action to rattle or drum for myself, but it was much easier, especially in the beginning, to use a CD or audiocassette of rhythmic, repetitive percussion. I found that I could access the visionary mode most easily while I was physically relaxed, preferably while lying down. But I could also do it while sitting up comfortably in a chair at home or in an airport, or propped against a tree in the woods, or even in my own backyard.

The CD that accompanies this booklet includes two 30-minute tracks of monotonous rhythm, one involving drumming, the other rattling. Some of us respond more strongly to the drum; others prefer the rattle. Each track includes about a half hour of steady rhythm, played at the rate of four to five beats or shakes per second.

This frequency corresponds to what neurophysiologists call the theta brain-wave rhythm, in which the human brain fires impulses at four to seven cycles per second. These slow, regular brain waves have been recorded in yogic practitioners and zen masters while in deep meditation. They're also the brain waves that have been recorded in some shamans while visioning, revealing that this vibrational tone of sound may be the "mouse" that double-clicks your program.

When I utilize the CD, I select either the rattling or drumming track, then I lie down on a blanket on the floor and close or cover my eyes with a bandanna or eye pillow. I listen to the sound, using either earphones or the "big set," then I focus my attention fully on my goals for the journey. These will be discussed shortly.

I then relax my physical body with a few clearing breaths, releasing any held tension. I settle into the sound of the rattle or the drum and instruct my subconscious

mind, or what the Hawaiians might call the "lower soul," to open the inner doorway located within it. This is where the portal into the spirit worlds is to be found. It's right there, within you, and it always has been.

✳ ✳ ✳   ✳ ✳ ✳

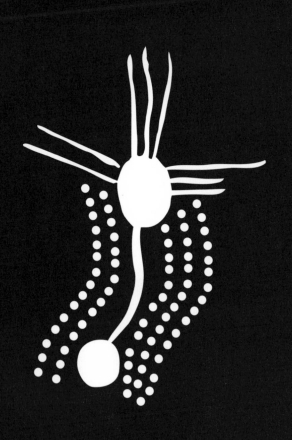

11 Opening the Portal

A Western-trained psychologist might affirm with confidence that such a personal, inner doorway is only there if you believe that it is. A traditional shaman might say with equal authority that the portal is already there, and it always has been, waiting for you to open it and travel through it into the inner worlds. I discovered its existence within myself quite by accident, so I tend to lean toward the indigenous view. Now, I simply listen to the drum or rattle and shift the primary focus of my conscious awareness from "here" to "there," wherever *there* happens to be. In response, the door obligingly opens, and off I go.

Allow me to put in here that the shaman, while in the visionary state, is always aware, to some degree, of what is going on around their physical body. This implies that you'll be able to hear the drum or rattle throughout your journey. This sound will carry you to your destination, and it will bring you back again. It will connect you to the spiritual realms as well as to your physical body. As long as you can hear the sound, you'll never get lost.

At the end of the journey, you'll hear a shift in tempo from the slower, steady monotonous beat into several minutes of more rapid percussion. You can use this shift in rythym as a cue to return the primary focus of your consciousness to your physical body. Accordingly, when you hear "the return," simply take leave of the visionary realms and intentionally shift your awareness back to your body in ordinary reality.

Remember, the sound of the drum or the rattle, not only double-clicks your program, but it's also a link between your "here" and your "there."

12 Protection

Before starting on a visionary journey, I always offer a short prayer to "the guys upstairs," or "TGU" as my friend Frank DeMarco likes to call them.[12] I'll say more about them toward the end of this book, but for now, let me say that I simply focus my awareness heavenward and ask the spirits "up there" to set my personal vibrational level on "high" so that no one of equal or lesser vibration can get into my field and mess with me or displace me. I always do this for basic protection when I'm going to be "out of my body."

Although you may not fully understand what "adjusting your vibrational level to high" means, the members of your "cosmic committee" in the Upper Worlds know exactly what this entails. And since they're always in connection with you—throughout your entire lifetime—your journey will then take place within a sphere of protection, extended toward you from those "on the other side of the mirror" who are compassionately concerned for you.

My protection prayer goes something like this:

"I offer my heartfelt greetings to the guys upstairs, and most especially to the members of my cosmic committee. I request that they provide me with power, protection, and support as I engage in spiritual fieldwork. I also ask that my vibrations be set on high, allowing my traveling soul to journey into the spiritual realms in complete safety, while my physical body awaits my return surrounded by a perimeter of protection. I offer my profound gratitude, as well as my respect, in advance. . . ."

Some of us also like to enhance our sense of spiritual protection with a visualization, such as surrounding our journeying self in a bubble of white light or a blue egg, or seeing ourselves held within the hands or wings of our guardian angel. Having done this simple protection ritual, I know with complete assurance that I'll be safe. This is most important, because spiritual work cannot be done in a state of fear.

I then take a couple of clearing breaths, relax into the sound of the rattle or the drum, and off I go.

13 Fine-Tuning the Method

Before using the CD, choose a time when you can be alone in your living space or wherever you are. If I'm at home, I usually select a period when my kids are at school—a time when I'm not tired or inclined to go to sleep. I also set myself up psychologically in advance by thinking about where I want to go and what I want to accomplish. Then, when the time comes, I simply lie down or sit comfortably, place the CD in the player and put on the earphones (if I'm using them), adjusting the sound to comfortable levels. Often I light a candle and some incense as a minimalist ritual.

I always begin my journeys by going to a place in the inner worlds I call my *sacred garden*. I'll discuss this locality shortly. During the journey, I simply remain in a suspended, relaxed state, allowing the steady resonance of the rattle or the drum to help maintain my focus "there." When I hear the "call back," I immediately shift my conscious awareness back to my physical body "here."

Allow me to repeat that during the exercise itself, you'll be aware to some degree of what's going on in your "here." You may perceive airplanes flying over your home, the dog barking next door, or the hum of the air conditioner or heater coming on. I try to minimize these distractions by turning off my cell phone and by taking the home phone off the hook so that my journey won't be interrupted in midstream.

When the journey is completed and the CD track has come to the end, I emerge from the expanded state and turn it off. I then spend as much time as is needed thoughtfully reviewing everything that was perceived during the exercise, making written notes to ensure that I won't forget what transpired.

Western-trained psychologists might categorize our shamanic journeys as fantasies, daydreams, or simply visualizations. They might conclude that we're just simply making the whole thing up with our creative imaginations. Or they might proclaim that it's our subconscious mind at work, filling in details, making the whole illusion more interesting.

And here is where I beg to differ.

Through my investigations of the inner worlds over the past 20 years, I've come to understand that the creative imagination is a function of the ego or conscious mind. But the journey takes place through what we call the subconscious, and this aspect of ourselves is not creative. Much like the hard drive of a computer, one of its primary functions is memory. Our subconscious is incapable of making anything up—it can only inform our conscious ego what it already knows or remembers. It can observe and perceive, however, and it can send what it has seen to our ego, which thinks about it, analyzes and categorizes it, and makes decisions about it.

Our subconscious is also the source of our feelings and emotions, and when we tap in to the feeling we have for a particular place, this confirms the subconscious to be the aspect of ourselves through which the journey is both experienced and perceived. Yet while we're in these subjective, dreamlike environments, our egoic inner director is receiving what we see, and it can still make decisions. The ego is involved, but as receiver, not perceiver; as director but not creator.

This reveals that you and I can determine the course of

the action to a certain extent with our egoic intentionality, but there comes a point when things begin to happen in the journey that we're not creating or intending. It is then that we've shifted into a level of reality and experience that has its own existence separate from ourselves. This is what it means to *vision*.

14 Recalling the Vision

When I first started doing shamanic journeywork, I would review the vision with focused concentration, and in the process of doing so, I often found that I seemed to remember far more than I was conscious of during the actual journey. This caused me to wonder if I was making it up. With continued practice, I concluded that I was not. Rather, I came to understand that my subconscious was disgorging everything that it had perceived, giving my conscious egoic mind the whole tamale, so to speak.

Reviewing and note-taking are thus revealed to be most important, as they are the keys to uncovering the subtleties and nuances within the greater picture that the journey is providing to you. In my own case, the ability to recall was elusive at first, but I found that it improved markedly with practice. If at first you don't seem to be remembering much, try again. Shamanic journeywork is a learned skill that improves with practice.

This intentional visionary fieldwork is the ancestral precursor of today's guided visualizations, hypnotherapy, or guided imagery therapies in which the therapist is verbally directing you through the experience or suggesting where to go or what to see or do. With shamanic journeywork, however, you're in control of the process from start to finish, creating your own objectives at the beginning, as well as your own goals for the journey, then allowing the vision to unfold on its own, providing you with information that you're perceiving, yet not creating.

When you open that portal, you're venturing into the inner worlds autonomously, as an explorer, supported by the vibration of the rattle, the drum, but without anyone directing the focus or content of your vision. In doing so, you're engaging in an ancient human experience—the ability to vision. And once your brain-mind complex gets what it is that you're after, you may be simply stunned by the elegant simplicity, as well as the power, of this time-tested method.

15 Ways of Perceiving

Some of us don't get those big-time visuals in seaching for our connection with the spiritual realms. Some receive information primarily through the auditory channel. Many musicians, actors, and psychic clairaudients often fall into this category. Such "audios" may actually enter the dream world through a sound, a vibration perhaps, or a "tone-poem" of beautiful, tranquil music in which information suddenly becomes available to them.

Others are very somatic in the way they access—they just know things, as though the information is coming to them through their body. Many psychics and clairsentients fall into this category, feeling and sensing their journeys rather than seeing them. Such inner travelers may tap in to a pervading sense of tranquility or peacefulness, and while in this state, they may simply receive information in response to their need to know.

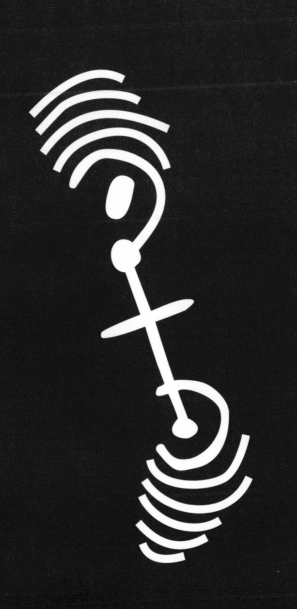

16 The Spiritual Realms

I t is of more than just passing interest that all shamans, in every society, perceive the spiritual realms in very much the same way—as a multilayered complex of subjective, dreamlike realities, existing simultaneously as levels of awareness on the one hand, and as levels of experience on the other.

By intentionally expanding their awareness in specific directions, shamans can effectively change their level of experience, in the process shifting from one level of reality to another. At the onset, we need a working outline about the nature of the spiritual worlds, as well as who and what we may encounter within them.

Located stratigraphically above the physical, everyday world that we all take so much for granted are the numinous, light-filled levels of the Upper Worlds. These are the sacred dimensions inhabited by the gods and goddesses, the spiritual heroes and heroines of the past, the higher angelic forces, and by those highly evolved powers beyond solar and planetary development. This is where the Heaven or Paradise of the transcendental monotheistic traditions may be found. And this is where each of us may find connection with our personal Oversoul or Higher Self.

If the visionary explorer wishes to make contact with the spirit of Jesus of Nazareth, the prophet Mohammed, Gautama the Buddha, Lord Krishna, Archangel Michael, or the Taoist Worthy Lao-Tzu, they would journey, with that intention, into the Upper Worlds in search of connection. And as the shamans and mystics of all traditions and all times have discovered, the Upper Worlds are where the spirit teachers reside.

Located below the physical plane of everyday existence are the Lower Worlds or Underworlds, encompassed and created by the great dreaming of Nature. These are the regions of adventure and power that have been visited by shamans for tens of millennia in order to connect with the spirits of the animals, the plants, the elementals, and even with the planet herself.

To visit with the spirits of Bear, Eagle, or Wolf; to

contact the spirits of Redwood, Oak, or Willow; or to connect with the spirit of Water, Fire, or the Earth herself, shamans across time have journeyed down into the Lower Worlds. All shamans know that one or more of these spirits may agree to come into relationship with you, serving as spirit helpers and allowing you to connect with the all-pervading energy that infuses everything everywhere with vitality and life-force.

In order to access these awesome inner worlds, the shaman's journeying soul usually passes through a passageway that often resembles a shimmering tunnel or tube. It can be short or long, depending on where one goes. This is the same tunnel leading from the darkness to the light that is so familiar to those who have had a near-death experience.

Shamans know about and have described this passage between the worlds, giving rise in virtually all cultures to the concept of an axis mundi or cosmic freeway system. One almost universal form for it is the great tree of life, whose roots lie in the Lower Worlds, whose trunk passes through the Middle Worlds, and whose crown emerges in the Upper Worlds. Another common form is the cosmic mountain that stands at the center of the Earth, at whose summit can be found the city of the Gods (Mount Olympus of the Greeks, for example).

Sometimes the axis of connection is perceived as a luminous grid, a great filamentous web or net or matrix that spreads out across the Universe, through which everything everywhere is interconnected with everything else. This is the Unitive Field of the mystic.

17 The Middle Worlds

I n between the Lower and Upper spiritual realms are found the Middle Worlds, which are dual in nature. On the one hand, there's the visible, objective plane of everyday physical reality. On the other, we find its nonvisible, nonordinary aspect, where the traditional peoples know we go during our dreaming while asleep.

Everything that exists in everyday, ordinary reality seems to have a spiritual aspect in this nonvisible, nonordinary middle world. Interestingly, I've heard many traditional people affirm with great confidence that we humans are actually dreaming 24 hours a day, and that this invisible dream world is all around us, all the time. The trick lies in learning how to perceive it while awake.

Shamans have mastered the ability to do this through their journeywork, in which they literally "dream while awake." Modern mystics and shamans proclaim with conviction that we human beings have actually created substantial portions of both the visible and nonvisible Middle Worlds through our dreaming and through our creative imagination.

These subjective, dreamlike realities of the Middle Worlds are of more than just passing interest to us, because this is where we find ourselves immediately following the death experience. The Bardo worlds of the Tibetans are located here, as are the after-death states of the Christian Purgatory. The Taoists have revealed that we may encounter the spirits of our ancestors in these dream worlds, as well as the souls of close friends, mates, and family members who have passed over within the last 100 years or so. This suggests that the souls of the dead can maintain their integration as a personal pattern for a substantial period of time.

It is also within the dreamlike levels of the Middle World that each of us may find our Sacred Garden—our personal place of power and healing.

This place can become a getaway within the other world, where we can retreat from the stresses and strains of everyday life in order to restore ourselves. This place can also serve as our cosmic gateway into the other spiritual levels of reality, awareness, and experience.

※ ※ ※　※ ※ ※

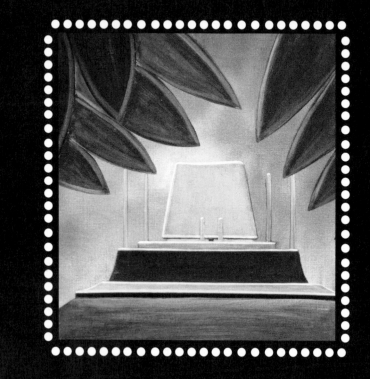

18 The Sacred Garden

I used to think of my own place of power and healing in the Middle Worlds as my "secret garden" because at one time, this place was known to me and no one else. Since I've chosen to write about experiences that occurred both within and through this place in my book *Visionseeker,* it's no longer a secret. And since we're dealing with the sacred realms, this locality could now be more accurately described as my "Sacred Garden." In discussing this with you, the reader, allow me to proclaim with absolute certainty that you have one, too. I'll elaborate.

All of us have fond memories of places that we've visited in life, places with which we feel a strong connection. Often these are localities in nature where we've felt complete somehow or at peace in ways that are hard to define, yet easy to feel. In our meditations or in our daydreaming, we often spontaneously reconnect with these places by simply remembering them, and by bringing up the feeling that we felt when we were there.

Those who have read my books know of my heartfelt connection with Hawai'i, and of how I learned to visit the Big Island by bringing up the memory of a beach at Kealakekua Bay where I used to swim every day with my wife and children. Over the years that I lived in the islands, I came to know every tree, plant, and stone of this locality, and when I returned to California, it was as though this place was inside me somehow. Through my shamanic journeywork, I discovered that I could go there in my dreaming-while-awake. My feeling for this place was my connection with it.

Accordingly, the dreaming of the beach at Kealakekua Bay came to serve as my Sacred Garden in my inner world, and through my visioning, I found, much to my amazement, that I could talk to the animals and the rocks in this place, as well as to the trees and the plants, the ocean and the wind. And they would respond, most often with non-verbal communication. But somehow, I could always understand what was "said" to me in ways that were elusive and mysterious, yet quite clear.

I discovered that I could do "gardenwork" in my garden, changing or altering the place according to how I wanted it to be. If I wished to have a bed of roses, a grove of mango trees, or a standing stone there, I just imagined them into existence, and they'd appear. If I wanted a waterfall to sit beside and rainbows to delight the eye, I dreamed them into existence. I even built a house in my garden and invited a caretaker to live in it when I wasn't there. Conversely, if I found something in my garden that I didn't want there, thorny vines growing all over everything, for example, or a swamp near my house, I could remove the vines or drain the swamp, even inviting in dream gardeners to help me do so.

And this is when I discovered something really interesting. When I changed my garden, something in my outer life would shift in response. It was almost as though everything in my garden was symbolic of some aspect of myself or my life experiences, and when I changed the symbols within my inner reality, something in my outer world changed, too. I have since come to accept that the ability to do this is magic—real magic.

※ ※ ※　　※ ※ ※

19 The Four Rules of the Garden

Through my inner explorations of this magical place across the years, I've discovered, as have countless others before me, that the Sacred Garden operates by four primary rules:

1. Everything in your garden is symbolic of some aspect of you or your life experience. This isn't surprising, since this is also the level of archetypes.

2. Everything in the garden can be communicated with to some degree, enhancing your understanding of both yourself and your life experiences. This practice is well known to the traditionals. We call it *divination.*

3. Everything in the garden can be changed so that it can be just the way you want it to be.

4. When you change your garden, some aspect of you or your life will change in response.

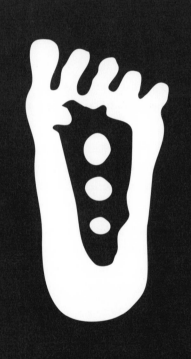

20 Finding Your Garden

I n searching for your garden, you might choose a locality in the everyday world that you already know and love—a pond in the woods where you caught turtles as a child, or a beautiful lagoon where you swam during a visit to a tropical island. You might be attracted to a forest of towering redwood trees along a foggy, wild coast, or to a magnificent valley surrounded by soaring mountains. You might be drawn toward the dry, mysterious baobab savannas of Africa; toward the endless steppes of Asia, dotted with horses and gazelles; or even to Central Park in New York City. Then again, it might just be the garden that's in your own backyard.

Your sacred garden can also be a purely imaginal place that you create for yourself, one that you can simply dream into existence using your intentions in tandem with your creative imagination. Many of us did this spontaneously as children, creating an inner world that sustained and nurtured us much like Peter Pan's adventurous Neverland, Alice's Wonderland, or Dorothy's Oz.

Much to my amazement, I've noted over the years that my Sacred Garden has the ability to change spontaneously, and it seems to do so independently of me or my intentionality. I was quite surprised the first several times this happened. This strongly suggests that the garden has an existence and a value that is separate from ourselves, and confirms yet once again that we're not making it all up.

I've also come to realize that all of us have such a personal place of power in the inner worlds of dream, and in sharing this information with you, I encourage each of you to find it. Your life may change dramatically in response, and much for the better. Once you have your garden set up just the way you want it to be, it will also be there for you when you make "transition."

This is because the garden is in the same spiritual level in which the after-death Bardo experience takes place. It's the level we go into when we graduate. Your garden can become your Bardo. . . .

My inner garden has become a place of great power and beauty in which I now do much of my spiritual work. I often invite my spirit helpers, as well as my spirit teacher, to meet with me there in order to accomplish various things. I've also discovered that this is a marvelous place to invite the spirits of my ancestors to visit, especially the ones who have passed over recently and who are still in transition.

Needless to say, it also gives me great satisfaction to know that I'll go to this wonderful place when I die, to accomplish my past-life review and to remain happily at ease until I'm ready to ascend and achieve reunion with my spiritual source-self, my oversoul.

※ ※ ※ ※ ※ ※

 21 Real Magic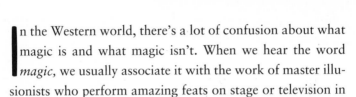

I n the Western world, there's a lot of confusion about what magic is and what magic isn't. When we hear the word *magic,* we usually associate it with the work of master illusionists who perform amazing feats on stage or television in front of bedazzled audiences.

The indigenous peoples know that real magic involves intentionally connecting with transcendent power and then manipulating, cajoling, or persuading it to assist in achieving some given end. Magic involves reaching through the mirror into the sacred realms, connecting with the power that resides there, and then bringing it back into this physical world in order to manifest something—such as healing, for example. That's magic.

※ ※ ※　※, ※ ※

79

22 Connecting with Power

In 1909, in a book called *The Threshold of Religion*, R. R. Marett proposed that the origins of spiritual awareness, and by association the origins of all organized religions, were to be found among the indigenous peoples' virtually universal belief in an impersonal, supernatural power that pervades and animates all things. Marett called this belief *animatism*.

A good example of animatism is to be found among the peoples of Polynesia, who attribute extraordinary events, unsual powers, and good fortune to the invisible force they call *mana*. This is analogous to the *manitou* of the Algonkians, the *baraka* of the Muslims, the *chi* of the Chinese, the *ki* of the Japanese and the Koreans, the *prana* of the Hindus, the *num* of the Kalahari bushmen, and *the Force* of Obi-Wan Kenobi.

Probably all people everywhere have a sense of this power. In the West, we tend to objectify it, associating it with localities such as Lourdes in southern France, or with objects like a sacred stone, a favorite pendant, or the good-luck charm on your key chain.

All indigenous peoples know that this power is widely dispersed throughout the universe, that it can be densely concentrated in certain places and objects, and that it infuses all beings with life force. Accordingly, all shamans and medicine people pay particular attention in learning how to maintain and even increase their personal supply because the effectiveness of all their practices is dependent on its presence as well as its "density." It's also understood that one's personal behavior, emotional habits, and mental attitudes can effect its ebb and flow, its abundance or its scarcity.

In Hawai'i, the main source of this energy for a person is known to be the *aumakua,* one's utterly trustworthy spiritual oversoul or "god-self" in the Upper Worlds. There are also, of course, the fields and currents of power that exist naturally within the physical environment, sources that we can connect with through our intentionality and focused concentration once we know how.

The belief in the existence of this power is one of the signatures of our consciousness age, and although most Westerners have to take this largely on faith, the shamans of the traditional peoples know with absolute certainty that this power is real. They also affirm that it may be transmitted by touch, that it can be absorbed through proximity, and that it may be harnessed for good or evil purposes depending on the intentions of those who can accumulate and manipulate it.

Our sacred garden in the Middle Worlds is our personal place of power. While there, we can intentionally increase our personal supply by paying close attention to our breathing accompanied by a visualization. While breathing slowly in to the count of four, visualize power streaming into the top of your head as a beam of light. Then, as you breathe slowly out to the count of four, see and feel the power descending through your head, neck, and chest, coming to rest within your third chakra in proximity to your navel. Four to eight breaths should be sufficient to enhance your power sufficiently. With practice, you can do this exercise anywhere and at any time, whenever there is a need.

※ ※ ※   ※ ※ ※

23 Making Magic in the Garden

O nce we become power-filled, we can use our creative imagination, a function of the egoic conscious mind, to make a thoughtform of something that we strongly desire to have or experience in our everyday reality. This is the first step to manifesting that something into our life. Remember the fourth rule of the garden—when you alter your garden, subtracting or adding something to that place, some aspect of you or your life will shift in response.

When you create something in your garden and then pay close attention to it every time you go there, your focused concentration causes energy to flow into the thoughtform. Energy flows where your attention goes, and with repetition, a strong energetic field will take form within and around the image—a field whose density will increase until it has the power to act as an energetic magnet that may attract the nearest available equivalent experience toward you in your outer life.

Remember—the more energy you have, the more you can accomplish. It is in this manner that all true magic works. Knowing this, you can create the perfect partner; that highly desired job; or perhaps a shift in your physical, mental, or emotional health, producing a miraculous healing from a supposedly incurable illness.

Let's take an example. Suppose you're suffering from something really serious, such as cancer, lupus, AIDS, or hepatitis C. You can go into your garden on a daily basis and connect with power. Then you can use whatever visualization you care to create to reverse the illness's effects and diminish its presence in your body. You might invite a spiritual healing master to come into your garden and work on you—or better yet, a *team* of healing specialists. Think of all the great healers across time—Imhotep, Aesclapius, Galen the Roman, Paracelsus, Jesus of Nazareth, the Medicine Buddha.

You can invite any or all of them to be on your team. When you're in your garden, you're right there in the spiritual worlds, and you can connect with these great souls.

It's amazing how often the spirit of Jesus of Nazareth

shows up in this capacity, offering healing through uncondi-
tional love, whether or not the sufferer is psychologically
Christian.[13] There are many compassionate spiritual healing
masters in all cultural traditions, and it is through them, and
through their connection with us, that we may penetrate to
the original cause of our affliction, neutralize its spiritual
aspect, and embark on our path of recovery with their full
and loving support.

You can ask them to restore your body to a state of balance and harmony, surrendering to their ministrations and
allowing yourself to experience their compassion for you,
and their healing power, in your time of need.

This brings us to consider the spirits . . . and most especially, those compassionate spirits who are willing to come
into relationship with us in order to help us in various ways.

24 The Garden As a Gateway

The garden is a perfect place through which to find connection with your spirit helpers and spirit teachers. These are the ones who are operating "behind the scenes," who hold you in high regard, and who have been supporting and protecting you ever since you were born into this life.

This doesn't mean that we don't have to go through stuff, and sometimes our life lessons can be very hard. But these spirits hold the keys to your well-being, your personal power, as well as your singular destiny. And once you invite them into your life, things can change, sometimes in quite dramatic ways.

The garden can be used as your gateway through which you connect with your spirit helpers, allowing your conscious awareness to travel into the levels of reality, awareness, and experience where they may be found. In doing so, I will next offer a few thoughtful suggestions for engaging in spiritual fieldwork.

✻ ✻✻ ✻✻ ✻

25 The Journey to the Lower Worlds

The spirit helpers tend to be found in the Lower Worlds. This generic term refers to the levels of the spiritual realms that have been created by the great dreaming of Nature, the regions of the dreamtime so familiar to mystics and shamans across the ages. Virtually all cultures have names for this place of power and adventure. The Hawaiians call it *Milu*.[14]

Begin your journey by saying your protection prayer, then go to your garden. Once there, refamiliarize yourself with this place and see if anything has changed since your last visit. Then search for an opening in the ground that leads down into the earth.

This portal might appear as a large cave in the hillside or a rabbit hole in the riverbank. It might be a hollow tree, a crack in the cliff, or even a tunnel just behind your waterfall. It could be an entrance through water, an undersea cave perhaps, or a submerged passage at the bottom of your sacred pool. Maybe it's a spiral staircase that leads down through an empty well-shaft, or it could be an elevator, much like the one in your apartment building.

However the portal appears to you, observe it closely while taking a couple of clearing breaths. Then simply go into it. The tunnel will be right there, just behind the opening, leading downward into the earth. Take courage and just go for it. Remember, you've just said your protection prayer and you're safe . . . and you're about to have a most important meeting, perhaps one that will change your life.

As you begin to proceed down the tunnel, put out a mental call in the form of a clear, conscious request for a spirit helper to be waiting for you in the Lower Worlds. Listen to the sound of the drum or rattle, and concentrate upon this objective, saying several times: "I wish to go to the Lower World to find my spirit helper." You may see vivid details of the tunnel walls, or you may just have a sense of passage through a dark place. Listen to the drum or rattle, and hold your focus.

The journey through the tunnel may be longer or shorter, depending on how far you're going. You may find yourself noticing holes in the tunnel wall. You may be drawn toward one of these holes and push right through it, or you may just find yourself moving toward a light at the tunnel's end. This hole or light is your doorway into the Lower World. Allow yourself to trust the experience. Remember, you're safe and are about to have a most interesting encounter.

When you emerge into the light, observe your surroundings closely. Inner travelers often perceive awesome and inspiring natural landscapes in vivid colors. Sometimes the natural beauty is simply overwhelming. If you have called for a spirit helper, 99 times out of 100, there will be someone or something waiting for you when you get there . . . and it may not be whom or what you're expecting.

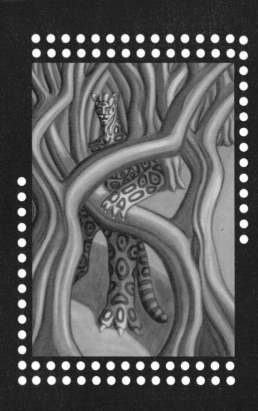

26 The Spirit Helpers

Your spirit helper may appear as that favorite animal for which you've always felt a strong attraction: the lion or the deer, the eagle or the serpent. It could also be a "mythical creature" such as a dragon or griffon, a unicorn or an elf. Such imaginal beings live in the Lower Worlds, and it is from these realms that they originally emerged into human consciousness. Their job is to supply you with power, protection, and support upon request. Our mythologies reveal that they've been doing this for humanity for a long time.

The frequency with which spirit helpers appear as animals, or as combinations of animal-human, has given rise to the term "power animal." But your spirit helper may also be a plant, the spirit of the oak or some other favorite tree, or perhaps a medicinal herb. It could be an elemental spirit such as the water woman, grandfather fire, the wind-keeper, or even the cosmic sun.

And speaking of grandparents, your spirit helper could just as easily be a wise old indigenous medicine woman or man, or even one of your own ancestors who has already passed over.

When you perceive the one waiting for you upon your arrival in the Lower Worlds, go up to it and ask it a yes/no question such as: "Are you here for me as a spirit helper?" The majority of the time, the spirit will indicate assent. That's why it's there, waiting for you.

The spirit helpers never lie to you, and if they say yes, you've scored—big time. You can now enter into relationship with this being, finding out who it is and how it communicates. You could ask it about some issue of importance. Maybe that's why it has come to you at this time—to convey this all-important information.

Whenever you ask a spirit a question, pay very close attention, because whatever happens next will be part of the answer. You may not get what you're expecting. Instead of clear, verbal answers, there may be memories that appear suddenly in your mind, or there may be thoughts and emotions that at first glance seem to be your own. Then, on reflection, you realize they're part of the answer that you have to figure out.

You might also ask your new spirit helper to take you on a tour of the Lower Worlds. You might be shown a particular place of power that you need to know about—a crystal cave or a beautiful temple, perhaps. Or you might simply find yourself in the most wondrous place you've ever seen.

Pay close attention and take mental notes. You're being shown the trails to places of power that will be there for you in the Other Worlds from this time forward. Sometimes you'll encounter yet another spirit there who wants to meet you, or perhaps a group of grandmothers or a council of grandfathers who have decided to come into relationship with you once again.

If the spirit you first encounter doesn't answer your question or says no (indicating it's not your helper), you can ask it to take you to your spirit helper or to point you in the right direction, and they will. If there's no one who seems to be waiting for you, take a walk and continue to put out the call. Sometimes a new helper will "flirt" with their human associate, coming and going, approaching and withdrawing, almost as if they're being shy or playful.

If something or someone is doing this with you, it's a good sign, and indicates that they're trying to get your attention. Sit down and wait, then simply indicate your wish to come into relationship with them. Ask if it would like to join you for a walk or a swim.

You may discover that you have more than one spirit helper. Traditional shamans collect spirit helpers because the more spirits they have, the more they can accomplish. Modern mystics do likewise. The helping spirits have qualities and abilities that distinguish them from each other. Some are great at providing protection; others may serve as guides or as sources of information; still others may help you with healing work. You'll discover what your spirits' abilities are through relationship with them.

When connecting with a new spirit helper, I always make a general request for power, protection, and support. With that intention established, I then begin to explore the nature of my relationship with this new spirit: "What are the goals that we may accomplish together? What qualities do you have that will be of service to me in doing healing work? How may I be of service to you in return? Why did you come to me?" These are some general suggestions for you to consider.

Rest assured that if you've made your protection prayer and asked specifically for a helping spirit, that's what your intentions will draw toward you. This means that you don't have to worry about any jokers or negative spirits showing up. You get what you ask for, and your spirit helpers may have been waiting around for a very long time for you to become aware of them and invite them back into your life once again. They have your well-being at heart, and one or more of them may have special knowledge about the nature of your personal destiny. If you ask them to do so, they may impart this knowledge to you.

※ ※ ※   ※ ※ ※

27 The Return

When you hear the "call back" on the CD, the rapid-fire drumming or rattling, take leave of your spirit friends and return back up the tunnel to your garden. From there, you may shift the focus of your attention back to your physical body. The garden thus serves as your point of departure as well as the place of return in all your spiritual journeys. As always, make detailed notes of the journey just completed.

Once in relationship with your spirit friends, you may invite them to meet with you in your garden. When confronted with an issue of importance or when dealing with a problem that someone else has invited you to work on (facilitating their healing, for example), you might have board meetings in your garden, bringing in all the spiritual others with whom you've established relationship. Often, someone new will show up in response to a particular need. I've created a special place in my garden in which to have these meetings.

※ ※ ※   ※ ※ ※

28 Spiritual Protocol

Rest assured that there *is* a spiritual protocol. This means that no spirit is allowed to interfere with you or your life unless you specifically invite them to do so. I sometimes feel uneasy when I hear someone say that "spirit is telling me to do this," or "spirit is directing me to go there." It has been my experience that no spirit helper will ever *tell* you what to do.

Exceptions do sometimes occur, but they usually involve miraculous avoidance experiences where a person is saved from an untimely accident or possible death that's not in accord with their life purpose. This happens because someone upstairs (or downstairs) is actively looking out for you, and given the emergency of the situation, they simply have to step in.

Prayer is another well-known and highly effective way of connecting with your helping spirits, especially in times of need. Prayer has been part of the technology of the sacred since the dawn of spiritual awareness. Prayer is the method by which we talk to the gods.

Your focused journeywork will allow you to take your relationships with the gods to a much deeper level, however. Whatever method you use, the protocol ensures that you're always the boss, that you're always the one in control. This is why the shaman is known in almost every culture as "the master of spirits."

29 The Journey to the Upper Worlds

The lofty spiritual realms above us include the localities known as Heaven or Paradise in the Judeo-Christian-Islamic traditions. These regions have been formed by the dreaming of the high goddesses, gods, spiritual heroes and heroines of the past, as well as the saints and prophets. Even those higher beings from beyond the beyond have contributed.[15]

These are also the levels where the higher angelic forces may be found. These multileveled regions are known as the Upper Worlds and are generally perceived as luminous and awe-inspiring realms of light. One or more of the beings that reside there may serve us as spirit teachers.

The commonly used term *guide* or *spirit guide* refers to the spirit teachers, not to the spirit helpers in the Lower Worlds. Exceptions do sometimes occur, since spirit helpers may serve us as teachers, especially in the beginning stages of our relationships with them.

Your spirit teacher in the Upper Worlds may be an ascended master, such as the patriarch Moses, Meyer Baba, Jesus, or even the Buddha. It may be your guardian angel or even your own higher self or oversoul. Most of us have one or more of our ancestors serving us as teachers as well.

There is also your cosmic committee, to be discussed shortly. To begin your journey, you might go to your garden and put out the call for one of your spirit helpers to provide you with assistance in traveling to the Upper Worlds. The goal: to meet with your spirit teacher.

Be aware that you may have more than one teacher, so you could be specific and ask for your "primary teacher," or you might express trust that you'll be brought into connection with the teacher who's just right for this time in your life.

The journey to the Upper Worlds can be particularly exhilarating, perhaps because the most common form of "out-of-body travel" to get there is through soul flight. The thing to remember is that it isn't the physical body that flies, it's your soul.

Once your intention to journey to your teacher is set, you

may allow yourself to be beamed up, drawn up, or simply taken up by someone who flies—the spirit of the hawk or the swan, for example. You may also find yourself merging with or even becoming an eagle, ascending on great soaring wing-beats into the vastness of the sky.

I've personally ridden on the back of a leopard more times than I can count, revealing that in the Other Worlds, terrestrial or aquatic creatures such as horses, leopards, dolphins, or sea turtles can fly. Aladdin's magic carpet and the magical broomstick used by the wise women of the woods are other ways that have been used to get there.

But sometimes, you just fly. . . .

There are different levels in the Upper Worlds, so as you listen to the drum or the rattle, try to keep track of how many levels you pass through before you arrive at your destination. As always, make detailed notes upon your return.

You're engaging in an extraordinary adventure, one that was experienced by traditional shamans and mystics tens of thousands of years before the rise of our organized religions. You're also rediscovering what it means to be fully human.

Some say that the gods gave us this gift so that we can

meet with them on their levels of reality, awareness, and experience. My spirit teacher has told me that the time has come for us to reclaim this gift, making it our own once again so that we may be drawn across that evolutionary threshold—and perhaps eventually become gods ourselves.

30 The Spirit Teacher

All of us have a primary spirit teacher in the Upper Worlds. This is an utterly trustworthy benevolent spirit-being who is in possession of all the knowledge and information that we might ever have need of during our lifetime here on Earth. Your teacher will share this wisdom with you upon request.

Sometimes your teacher will simply respond to your need to know by sending you dreams or visions. Perhaps ideas or hunches will appear suddenly within your mind at just the right time, or you may suddenly "know" just what to do. This reveals that your spirit teacher is the source of what we call our "intuition."

Your spirit teacher may also take a more active role in your life, and you may be "guided" to be present at a certain lecture, meet a certain person, or take a certain workshop that will provide you with just what you need to know. Such experiences reveal that our spirit teacher is in touch with us throughout your life (or lives), and can manifest effects such as nudging you in just the right direction, at just the right time.

My teacher usually answers my requests for information by offering me a spread of all the various possiblities and options to be considered. It is in this way that my teacher consistently demonstrates that there are always choices, and that the choice is always mine to make.

It has been my experience that the spirit teacher never tells you what to do, but he/she will provide you with information and guidance revealing "how" you may proceed or "what" you might do in response to this or that situation.

How you word your requests to your teacher is obviously important in this regard. I've found that "should" questions don't work well, such as "Should I do this or should I do that?" These don't yield good results because it's the job of your conscious, egoic decision maker to make choices. And the choices that it makes, in full awareness or not, are what draw us further and further along the path of power and beauty . . . or its opposite.

Questions that begin with "What," "When," "How," and "Why" tend to provide us with much clearer answers. For example: "*What* are the issues that need to be clarified around this relationship?" or "*How* may I proceed in resolving this problem?" The answer may come this way: "*What* you need to do is . . ."

Once again, when you ask a question, pay very close attention to whatever happens next. A series of memories may appear in your mind, or you may perceive imagery that at first glance has seemingly nothing to do with your question. These are often symbolic ways in which the teacher chooses to communicate with you, providing information as well as lessons to be learned. With reflection, the answer usually becomes obvious. That's your job: to figure it out.

You may also invite your teacher to join you in your garden. Accordingly, you might consider creating a special place there where such meetings might be held.

Although I love to go to the Lower and Upper Worlds, I now do much of my spiritual work in my garden, a place of refuge and tranquility to which I have instant access, whenever there's a need. Needless to say, my spirits love my garden, and I'll often arrive to find that the one I wish to connect with is already there.

The vibrations of the drum and the rattle are powerful tools that may assist you in finding connection with your garden, your helpers, your teachers, and even with your ancestors. They are just there at the edge of your awareness, waiting to be of service to you. All you have to do is turn in their direction . . . and the rest then happens by itself.

With continued practice, you'll find that you may be able to accomplish this simply through your intentionality alone, and that you no longer need these physical stimuli. This, of course, is the goal of continued, sustained practice—to have instant access to our inner sources of power and wisdom upon request. Some of us have achieved this ability in previous lifetimes, and so many psychics, for example, or those with advanced intuitive abilities, are already there.

Through the use of the journeywork method, enhanced by the drum or rattle, we also discover that we're never truly alone. All of us have a constellation of spiritual helpers and teachers who are behind us, around and below us, and even hovering over us . . . all the time. The trick lies in learning to perceive them.

These allies have our very best interests at heart, yet they never judge, never condemn, never criticize. They know that there's no such thing as constructive criticism. There are only lessons. And because we have life lessons to learn, things happen. It's in response to those lessons that we become who and what we are.

Once we invite our spirit helpers and teachers back into our lives, asking them to provide us with guidance and wisdom, power and protection, information and support, the whole game of life changes. At this point, our lives—our own personal slice of the great mystery of existence—may become an immeasurably enriched adventure.

31 Your Life's Purpose

I n the mid-1960s, I lived for two years as a Peace Corps
volunteer among the Yoruba peoples of Nigeria, and it
was there that I first witnessed something I didn't fully
comprehend. It was only years later, when I had seen it
among other tribal peoples in southern Ethiopia and eastern
Africa, that understanding came.

Among these traditional peoples, when a woman
expecting a child enters the last trimester of her pregnancy,
the shamans of her community approach her, and with her
permission, they place her in a deep state of trance. The
shamans then connect with the spirit of the child coming
into life, and they speak to it, requesting that it reply using
the mother's voice. The shamans' questions are riveting:
"Who are you? Why are you coming into our village? What
is your life purpose?"

In this manner, the village learns who's coming in and
why, and this is important for the community as well as the

child. During adolescence, for example, when the teenager is driven by natural contrariness and by the need to individuate, that individual may stray from their path. The whole village knows who they are, however, and what their life pupose is, and so the community can gently steer that person back in the right direction.

It's in this way that harmony and balance is maintained and furthered—in the individual as well as in the community. It's in this manner that disharmony and dis-ease, which includes illness, is kept within bounds.

While this custom may seem strange, even outlandish, to Western peoples, I suspect that it may be very much part of the given for traditional societies everywhere. It may be that it was once part of our heritage as well. But there's another aspect of this dynamic that is of great interest. . . .

32 The Cosmic Committee

The words spoken by the child's spirit also suggest that the incoming individual has submitted a proposal for the life-way to be lived to a council of elder spirits. And it's on the basis of this proposal that the newcomer is given permission to be born into this world, to inhabit a physical body here on the plane of action, and to become part of the community.[16]

The implication is that each one of us has such a spiritual council, a cosmic committee, if you will, who gave us permission to be born. This cluster of "elder spirits" is very much aware of what our life's purpose is, and they're monitoring our life as we live it, silently applauding us as we achieve our life's goals, silently feeling concern as we fail in our tasks. This insight implies that privacy is truly an illusion . . . and that we are never, ever alone.

※ ※ ※   ※ ※ ※

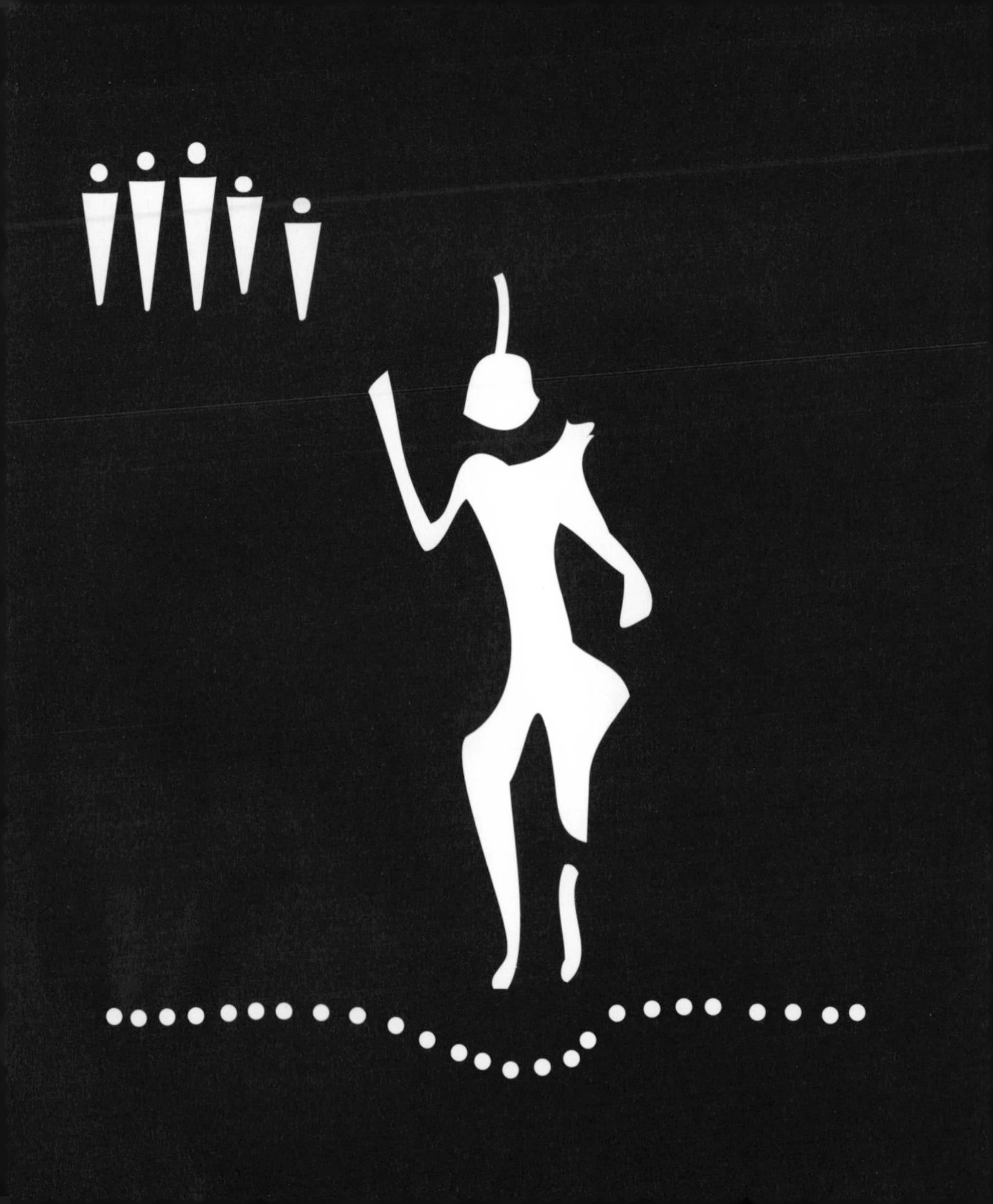

33 The Contract

This revelation also implies that each one of us has a cosmic contract upon which we ourselves have written the shape and nature of our life's purpose for this time around, and possibly many lifetimes to come.

We can use our shamanic journeywork to reconnect with our cosmic committee, traveling to meet with them in the Upper Worlds, or we can actually invite them into our garden.

Once in connection with our council of spirit elders, we may actually review the terms of our cosmic contract. It is in this way that:

- we can learn the true nature of our life's purpose, and

- we can reaffirm that which we agreed to do in this life.

We can also renegotiate the terms of our contract.

Whenever we feel lost or confused, or when we feel that we've somehow strayed from our path, it's my gentle suggestion that we make a journey to our garden and invite our committee to come in for a meeting.

These elder spirits know who you are and what you're here for. They are members of your spiritual family, and it's through them that you may discover paths into understanding the nature of yourself, the nature of this reality, as well as the nature and shape of your trail through this life. You may even get glimpses into many of your lifetimes, both past and future, giving you greater insights into who you really are.

As I, the writer, create these words, and as you, the reader, read them, I perceive the nodding assent of uncountable unseen allies, and I know with absolute certainty that there's much richness to be explored here (more nods).

34 The Ascent

ecent surveys have revealed that as many as one in every two of us has had an involuntary paranormal experience at some point in our lives—one that has carried us across some unknown inner threshold into the more expanded realms of consciousness.

This confirms my suspicion that when each of us becomes aware of that bioenergetic program that exists within us, when we awaken from the consensus slumber of culture at large and remember that we were once seeds of light, traveling among the stars, accompanied and protected by spiritual guardians (another story for another time), each of us can use the spiritwalker program we possess as a guide, as a map. We can then use this map to navigate our way through the forests of illusion and across the plains of experience.

As we awaken, our life experiences can begin to manifest themselves as a true hero's journey, as an upward quest that leads us inevitably into direct experience of the spiritual realms. Those who have already achieved this know that this journey becomes possible for us only through the doorway of the heart.

It is through this gateless gate that we, as individuals, can personally experience connection with unlimited power and a godlike mind. We know then, with absolute certainty, that no holy words or books, no secret ceremonies and rituals, no spiritual leaders or gurus or faiths can do this for us.

Once the spiritwalker program is activated and the higher evolutionary functions are triggered, a predetermined schedule is set into motion, one that cannot be given to us by any outside agency.

This is because each one of us already has it.

The paths that we take through life are the vehicles through which we awaken. So as each of you proceeds on with your life, growing, increasing, and becoming more, please take these thoughts with you . . . with my gratitude and my warmhearted aloha.

— **Hank Wesselman**

✵ ✵ ✵   ✵ ✵ ✵

Notes

1. Current research has shown, for example, that the physical structure of the brain can be rearranged in as little as 15 minutes in response to the process of learning. See Daniel Weinberger, Douglas W. Jones, and Alicia Bartley's paper "Genetic Variability of Human Brain Size and Cortical Gyral Patterns," in *Brain*, vol. 120: pp. 257–269 (1997).

2. Others have also explored these interesting insights. See, for example, Yatri's *Unknown Man: The Mysterious Birth of a New Species* (New York: Fireside Books, 1988).

3. See Ralph Metzner's *Green Psychology: Transforming our Relationship to the Earth* (Rochester, Vermont: Park Street Press, 1999); and his *Ayahuasca: Human Consciousness and the Spirits of Nature* (New York:

Thunder's Mouth Press, 1999). See also Susana
Valadez's paper "Sacred Plants and the Goddess,"
in *Candlemas*, 1990.

4. See Roger N. Walsh, *The Spirit of Shamanism*
    (Los Angeles: Jeremy P. Tarcher Press, 1990)
    for an overview.

5. See Richard Katz, *Boiling Energy: Community
    Healing Among the Kalahari Kung* (Cambridge and
    London: Harvard University Press, 1982). For indige
    nous perspectives on shamanic experience, see Joan
    Halifax, *Shamanic Voices: A Survey of Visionary
    Narratives* (New York: Dutton, 1979).

6. See Hank Wesselman's *Spiritwalker: Messages
    from the Future* (New York: Bantam Books, 1995);
    *Medicinemaker: Mystic Encounters on the Shaman's
    Path* (New York: Bantam Books, 1998); and
    *Visionseeker: Shared Wisdom from the Place of
    Refuge* (Carlsbad, California: Hay House, 2001).

7.   Michael Harner and I have discussed this at some
     length. See his book *Way of the Shaman:*
     (San Francisco: Harper, 1990).

8.   Roger Walsh, p. 24; and Chapter 1 in *Visionseeker.*

9.   These words were written by a learned Cambridge
     graduate named Henry More in the early 1600s.
     Those interested in the witches as healers should
     read Jeanne Achterberg's *Imagery in Healing:
     Shamanism and Modern Medicine* (Boston and
     London: Shambhala New Science Library, 1985).

10. I acknowledge here my debt to Michael Harner.
     Without his wise guidance and accomplished teach-
     ings, the shamanic skills and abilities of thousands of
     people, including myself, might have remained unde-
     veloped and their spiritwalker program misdiagnosed
     (i.e., pathologized). His Foundation for Shamanic
     Studies' Website can be accessed at:
     www.shamanism.org.

11. For a thoughtful overview of the beliefs and trends
held dear by the awakening evolutionary sleepers, see
Medicinemaker, pp. 216–222, and my essay on The
Modern Mystical Movement at: **www.sharedwisdom.com**.
See also Paul H. Ray and Sherry Ruth Anderson's *The
Cultural Creatives: How 50 Million People Are Changing
the World* (New York: Harmony Books, 2000).

12. See Frank DeMarco, *Muddy Tracks: Exploring
an Unsuspected Reality* (Charlottesville, Virginia:
Hampton Rhodes, 2001).

13. See Chapter 17 in *Visionseeker* for a dramatic example.

14. Allow me to observe that the Lower Worlds are not
a realm of pain and suffering called Hell. It is most unfor-
tunate that during the Middle Ages, the priesthoods of
the emerging church felt the need to demonize the Lower
Worlds, much like they demonized the witch-healers.
Perhaps this was done to instill fear and keep people from
going there in vision, effectively separating them from
their power, protection, and support. This, of course,

created a co-dependent relationship between them and the church.

It was also during this time that Satan, the fallen angel, acquired horns and hooves, effectively demonizing Cernunnos, the antlered or horned god of Nature and the lord of the animals who was so revered by the pre-Christian European peoples. As the esteemed mythologist Joseph Campbell put it, when a new religion replaces an old one, the gods of the old religion become the demons in the new.

15. From my perspective, articulated in *Visionseeker,* pp. 285–287, the existence of a supreme creator-God, whose intentionality set the whole process of creation into motion, is unknown. Despite various well-intentioned religious belief systems and claims to the contrary, the actuality of a divine Creator is, and will forever be, the Great Mystery—the *mysterium tremendum.* Connection with the divine field, The Source of All Being, is possible however. See *Visionseeker,* Chapter 16.

16. For confirmation, see Malidoma Patrice Somé's *The Healing Wisdom of Africa: Finding Life Purpose through Nature, Ritual, and Community* (New York: Jeremy P. Tarcher/Putnam, 1999).

Shamanic Training Workshops

Interest in shamanic training workshops
with Hank Wesselman and his wife, Jill Kuykendall,
can be directed to:

e-mail: hank@sharedwisdom.com
Website: **www.sharedwisdom.com**

※ ※ ※　※ ※ ※

About the Author

Anthropologist **Hank Wesselman, Ph.D.**, is one of those rare cutting-edge scientists who truly walks between the worlds. He did his undergraduate work, as well as his master's degree, in zoology at the University of Colorado at Boulder, then went on to get his doctoral degree in anthropology from the University of California at Berkeley.

Hank served in the U.S. Peace Corps in the 1960s, living among people of the Yoruba Tribe in Western Nigeria, where he became interested in indigenous spiritual traditions. Since the early 1970s, he has conducted research with an international group of scientists, exploring eastern Africa's Great Rift Valley in search of answers to the mystery of human origins. This has allowed him to spend much of his life with traditional peoples.

His autobiographical books *Spiritwalker, Medicinemaker,* and *Visionseeker* are focused upon an ongoing continuum of visionary experiences that began spontaneously out in the bush of southern Ethiopia in the 1970s, resumed in Hawai'i in the 1980s, and continue to the present day. Combining the sober objectivity of a trained scientist with a mystic's passionate search for deeper understanding, Hank's books and teachings contain revelations about the nature of the self, the nature of reality, as well as the nature of the spiritual worlds.

Hank has taught for the University of California, San Diego; the University of Hawai'i at Hilo's West Hawai'i Campus; California State University at Sacramento; American River College; Sierra College; and also for Kiriji Memorial College and Adeola Odutola College in Nigeria. He currently offers seminars and training workshops at many internationally recognized centers such as the Esalen Institute in California and the Omega Institute near New York.

Other Hay House Titles of Related Interest

Books

Contacting Your Spirit Guide,
by Sylvia Browne (book and CD)

*Crossing Over,
by John Edward

Getting in the Gap,
by Dr. Wayne W. Dyer
(book and CD)

Messages from Your Angels,
by Doreen Virtue

Meditation, by Brian L. Weiss, M.D.
(book and CD)

*Published by Princess Books; distributed by Hay House

Mirrors of Time,
by Brian Weiss, M.D.
(book and CD)

Sacred Ceremony,
by Steven D. Farmer, Ph.D.

Secrets & Mysteries, by Denise Linn

Turning Inward
(a journal for self-reflection),
by Cheryl Richardson

Audio Programs

Intuitive Healing,
by Judith Orloff, M.D.

Journeys into Past Lives,
by Denise Linn

Karma Releasing,
by Doreen Virtue

*Understanding Your Angels
and Meeting Your Guides,*
by John Edward

※ ※ ※   ※ ※ ※

All of the products listed on the previous pages
are available at your local bookstore,
or may be ordered through Hay House, Inc.
at the address on the next page.

☀ ☀ ☀   ☀ ☀ ☀

We hope you enjoyed this Hay House book. If you'd
like to receive our online catalog featuring additional
information on Hay House books and products, or if you'd
like to find out more about the Hay Foundation, please contact:

Hay House, Inc., P.O. Box 5100, Carlsbad, CA 92018-5100
(760) 431-7695 or (800) 654-5126
(760) 431-6948 (fax) or (800) 650-5115 (fax)
www.hayhouse.com® • www.hayfoundation.org

Published and distributed in Australia by: Hay House Australia Pty.
Ltd., 18/36 Ralph St., Alexandria NSW 2015 • *Phone:*
612-9669-4299 • *Fax:* 612-9669-4144 • www.hayhouse.com.au

Published and distributed in the United Kingdom by: Hay House UK,
Ltd., 292B Kensal Rd., London W10 5BE • *Phone:* 44-20-8962-1230
Fax: 44-20-8962-1239 • www.hayhouse.co.uk

Published and distributed in the Republic of South Africa by:
Hay House SA (Pty), Ltd., P.O. Box 990, Witkoppen 2068
Phone/Fax: 27-11-467-8904 • www.hayhouse.co.za

Published in India by: Hay House Publishers India, Muskaan
Complex, Plot No. 3, B-2, Vasant Kunj, New Delhi 110 070 • *Phone:*
91-11-4176-1620 • *Fax:* 91-11-4176-1630 • www.hayhouse.co.in

Distributed in Canada by: Raincoast, 9050 Shaughnessy St.,
Vancouver, B.C. V6P 6E5 • *Phone:* (604) 323-7100
Fax: (604) 323-2600 • www.raincoast.com

Take Your Soul on a Vacation

Visit www.HealYourLife.com® to regroup, recharge,
and reconnect with your own magnificence. Featuring blogs,
mind-body-spirit news, and life-changing wisdom
from Louise Hay and friends.

Visit www.HealYourLife.com today!

☀ ☀ ☀   ☀ ☀ ☀